A Williamsburg Christmas

Garnished with a sprig of holly, a pecan tart, the most traditional of all southern desserts, is featured on a walnut dresser in the Brush-Everard Kitchen. Antique pewter softly reflects the candle's glow.

THE WORLD OF WILLIAMSBURG

A Williamsburg Christmas

PHOTOGRAPHS BY FRANK J. DAVIS AND ROBERT LLEWELLYN
TEXT BY DONNA C. SHEPPARD
DRAWINGS BY VERNON WOOTEN

The Colonial Williamsburg Foundation
Williamsburg, Virginia

Hardbound edition distributed by Holt, Rinehart and Winston, New York, N. Y.
Distributed simultaneously in Canada by Holt, Rinehart and Winston of
   Canada, Limited

Library of Congress Cataloging in Publication Data
Sheppard, Donna C
     A Williamsburg Christmas.
       1. Williamsburg, Va.—Social life and customs—Pictorial works.
2. Williamsburg, Va.—Description—Views. 3. Christmas—Virginia—
Williamsburg—Pictorial works. [1. Christmas—Virginia—Williamsburg.
2. Williamsburg, Va.—Description. 3. United States—Social life and
customs—Colonial period, ca. 1600-1775]
I. Davis, Frank J.   II. Llewellyn, Robert, 1945-   III. Title.
IV. Series: World of Williamsburg.
F234.W7S52   975.5′4252043   80-17179

ISBN 0-87935-053-9 Hardbound
ISBN 0-87935-054-7 Softbound

This book was designed by Vernon Wooten
PRINTED IN THE UNITED STATES OF AMERICA

Poem on page 1 courtesy of the Tucker-Coleman Papers, Earl Gregg Swem
   Library, College of William and Mary, Williamsburg, Va.

917.554252
SHE

Good people all, the Season comes
For Christians to be merry:
School Boys, with Hobby-horse & Drums,
Old Men, with Sack and Sherry.
When Housewives treat with hot mincepies
And Planters, with good Cyder.

The Christmas season in Williamsburg, the restored capital of His Majesty's royal colony of Virginia, is festive indeed. Candles gleam in every window and good things to eat and drink abound. Pungent wood smoke adds its unique fragrance to the crisp winter air. A delightful sense of anticipation is felt everywhere as townspeople and visitors alike prepare for the gala celebrations of this special holiday. There are decorations to create and display, special foods and beverages to bake and brew, age-old carols to sing, and tunes for fiddling and toe tapping.

Christmas in eighteenth-century Virginia was above all a family time. Relatives and friends gathered from near and far to exchange the latest news and gossip and just enjoy being together. Crops had been safely gathered in, and the fertile fields of the Old Dominion rested under a light dusting of snow. The master and mistress took time from their busy rounds to keep Christmas, the happiest and most holy moment of the year.

That the hospitable Virginians enjoyed the conviviality of the Christmas holidays was noted in his diary by Philip Vickers Fithian, tutor to the children of Robert Carter at Nomini Hall plantation. "Nothing is now to be heard of in conversation, but the *Balls,* the *Fox-hunts,* the fine *entertainments,* and the *good fellowship,* which are to be exhibited at the approaching *Christmas.*"

December 25 was observed primarily as a holy day. The entire family worshipped in the parish church and took the sacrament. Servants and laborers enjoyed a day of rest. Some of them may have received small gifts of money, food, or clothing. Santa Claus, or Saint Nicholas, the jolly man in red whose reindeer-drawn sleigh arrives

1

with presents for good boys and girls, had not yet become a part of the folklore of Christmas; the first decorated tree appeared in Williamsburg only in 1842. But the spirit of Christmas, of good fellowship and hospitality, was as ever-present then as it is today.

The Grand Illumination of the City ushers in the Christmas holidays in Williamsburg. Bonfires are lit at several locations in the Historic Area, while tall cressets help illuminate the festivities. Cannons boom and firing exercises by the artillery and musketmen signal the opening of the evening's program. The Fife and Drum Corps joins in as they parade along Duke of Gloucester Street. There is music and activity everywhere—dancers in colonial costumes turn and twirl to the tunes of a fiddle, madrigal singers perform favorite eighteenth-century airs, the wail of a bagpipe punctuates the night air. White tapers twinkle in each window, their cheery glow enhancing the holiday mood. Visitors and townspeople mingle as they sing their favorite traditional carols and exchange merry Christmas greetings. The Grand Illumination concludes with fireworks, a fitting way to celebrate the beginning of the Christmas season.

Members of the Senior Fife and Drum Corps herald the season with traditional tunes—"Successful Campaign," "King of Denmark's March," and "Soldier's Wedding." Cressets, fueled with pitch pine, burn as brightly as they did two centuries ago.

2

Candles glow in every window of the Peyton Randolph House, home of the first president of the Continental Congress. A twilight hush settles over the old city, and footsteps of long ago seem to echo in the quiet streets.

The Courthouse of 1770 has stood watch over Market Square for more than two hundred years.

Duke of Gloucester Street at dusk.

Dancing has long been a favorite pastime for Virginians of all ages. The eighteenth-century **Virginia Gazette** contained many advertisements by Williamsburg dancing masters who proposed to teach their pupils "in the neatest and newest manner." At the Grand Illumination, young dancers swing their partners through the familiar steps of a reel.

6

The fiddler's merry music provides a sprightly accompaniment to the dancing.

Students, visitors, and townspeople gather in the College yard to hear a special Christmas message. Chartered by the king and queen of England in 1693, the College of William and Mary is the second oldest institution of higher learning in the country. Its venerable Wren Building, at one end of Duke of Gloucester Street, is illuminated for the holidays.

Completed in 1733, the President's House has been the residence of all but one president of the College.

7

Traditional matching wreaths of greens with mixed fruit decorate the divided door on the John Carter Store.

8

The holly and the ivy.
When they are both full grown.
Of all the trees that are in the wood.
The holly bears the crown.

Decorations are an important part of a Williamsburg Christmas. Tinsel and foil are eschewed, and the emphasis is on those plant materials—fruits, greens, cones, seed pods, and nuts—that were available to eighteenth-century Virginia housewives.

Inspired by the terra cotta sculptures of the della Robbias and the wood carvings of Grinling Gibbons, today's wreaths feature imaginative arrangements of such traditional or exotic fruits as apples, lemons, limes, pineapples, pears, pomegranates, and kumquats. Natural materials like the dried pods of okra, magnolia, and milkweed, sweet gum balls, bayberry and chinaberry, nuts, cotton bolls, mistletoe, and various pine cones are used extensively. Holly, nandina, and pyracantha berries add a touch of red. Greens—ivy, cedar, balsam, pine, boxwood—are combined with the leaves of magnolia, aucuba, or camellia to create pleasing effects.

Decorations may be as elaborate as a carefully constructed fan of matched apples topped with a pineapple, the traditional symbol of hospitality, over the door of an impressive red brick residence or as simple as a charming tiny spray of pine and holly on the windowsill of a modest shop. Elaborate or simple, plain or fancy, each decoration in Williamsburg's Historic Area expresses the spirit of Christmas then and now.

9

White pine roping and a boxwood wreath with pomegranates adorn the gate of the Governor's Palace. Chiseled in stone, the English lion and the Scottish unicorn flank the gilded wrought-iron crown of England and cypher of Queen Anne. A wreath and candle accent each window of the elegant residence of seven royal governors and the first two elected governors of the Commonwealth of Virginia, Patrick Henry and Thomas Jefferson.

Above left. *The door of a private residence bears a boxwood wreath with lemons, sliced osage oranges, aucuba leaves, and cotton bolls.*

Above. *Framed by white pine and backed by magnolia leaves, a cornucopia basket spills lemons, oranges, holly berries, and juniper.*

A boxwood wreath with red cedar, holly berries, and apples brightens the window of the John Blair Kitchen. Below, the basket holds an arrangement of red cedar, apples, bayberry, and holly.

11

An eager group of children on a Tricorn Hat Tour pause to admire a colorful doorway. A hostess describes the decorations.

12

Above left. *One of a matching pair on a private residence, this plaque combines magnolia and boxwood with artichokes and yellow apples.*

Above right. *White pine roping surrounds the fanlight at the federal period Norton-Cole House, while the boxwood wreath on the pine-roped railing features a geometric treatment of lemons and limes accented by bayberry.*

Left. *The transom above the door of the George Wythe House is emphasized by white pine roping and a boxwood wreath with bright red apples and American holly berries. Red holly berries tucked in each corner above the door repeat the colorful theme.*

13

The boxwood wreath at the Coke-Garrett House is dressed with pomegranates, lemons, oranges, lady apples, magnolia pods, and pyracantha berries. White pine roping defines the doorway.

"On the first day of Christmas, my true love gave to me, a partridge in a pear tree." A modern interpretation of the favorite carol features real pears nestled in a boxwood tree. The partridge has been created from pine cone scales.

Pears, apples, lemons, pine cones, and sumac appear on a boxwood wreath fashioned in two sections. White pine roping with a touch of holly frames the doorway.

14

*White pine roping outlines
the entry of the William
Lightfoot House; a box-
wood wreath with a
traditional fruit treatment
and a red velvet bow
centers the door.*

15

Above. *Natural materials such as chinaberries, bayberry, statice, piñon pine cones, and black pine cones cut into rosettes grace a white pine wreath. The burlap bow adds the finishing touch.*

Above right. *A stylized interpretation on a private residence radiates from an artichoke surrounded by a cluster of holly berries and features a ring of kumquats outlined by alternating white pine cones and yellow apples centered by cranberries, all backed with magnolia leaves.*

A wreath of white pine to which magnolia leaves, clusters of cones, red and yellow apples, lemons, and a lime or two have been affixed complements a brass door knocker.

The crisp red bow adds a bright splash of color to pine roping on a wrought-iron railing.

17

Above. *A pineapple, the traditional symbol of hospitality that dates from colonial days, is the focal point of a fan of crisp red apples arranged on boxwood and magnolia leaves above the door at the Robert Carter North Quarters.*

Far right. *The transom and banister of the Ludwell-Paradise House are garlanded with roping of white pine mixed with holly.*

Cookies tied with gay red ribbons add a festive touch to a boxwood wreath.

A spray of apples, boxwood, and magnolia under the windowsill at the Robert Carter North Quarters further carries out the theme.

In the winter chill, busy craftspeople hurry to their shops without pausing under the ribbon-bedecked boxwood kissing ball that hangs beside the Waters-Coleman House.

The impressive Ludwell-Paradise House wreath of red and yellow apples and Maine wild crab apples highlights the transom.

19

Above. *Sliced osage oranges, kumquats, okra pods, and rose hips decorate a balsam wreath on a private residence.*

Above right. *Lady apples and scrub pine cones centered on a plaque of scrub pine and magnolia leaves create a simple yet pleasing effect.*

The windowsill at the Music Teacher's Shop bears an arrangement of white pine and white pine cones, okra and iris pods, and red and lady apples.

Matching boxwood wreaths are trimmed with red apples, okra pods, cotton bolls, pine cones, and clusters of rose hips.

Mountain laurel, boxwood, cut pine cones, and sumac enhance a pair of white pine wreaths.

The horse-drawn yellow wagon carries visitors past the Archibald Blair House, which stands on Market Square green.

Above left. *Pyracantha on the south wall of the Norton-Cole House steals the show.*

Above. *A live oak tree frames Christmas wreaths on the President's House at the College of William and Mary.*

A boxwood plaque by the door of the John Greenhow House West includes cherry laurel, lemons, lavender, bits of yarrow, and a perfect pineapple.

23

White pine wreaths and boxwood gar-
landing combine to form pleasing
patterns on the Robert Carter House.

The Brush-Everard House door greets
the season with a wreath of multi-
colored chinaberries, lotus pods,
sweet gum balls, cotton bolls, pine
cones, and lemons and limes.

24

Simple boxwood wreaths accent the window at the Margaret Hunter Shop.

25

26   *The late afternoon sun gilds the steeple of Bruton Parish Church; leafless branches weave a canopy overhead.*

27

*A tranquil view of Duke of Gloucester Street
from the Bruton Parish Church tower.*

An apple cone spiked with box-wood makes an ideal centerpiece for a holiday table.

28

A bright green lime surrounded by candied orange peel and marzipan strawberries tops a pyramid of glass salvers on which antique porcelain birds, glasses of mint jelly, and sprigs of holly and white pine have been placed. The table dividers feature fresh limes, holly berries, sprigs of boxwood and pine, and small dishes filled with lady apples and red and green grapes. A pecan tart completes the setting.

Tossing the ball up and trying to catch it on the stake of a "bilbo-catcher" has been a popular pastime for children down through the years. An antique doll watches the fun.

29

Above left. *An elaborate arrangement of fruits, nuts, and leaves decorates the table in the dining room at Carter's Grove plantation. Claret punch and a tempting assortment of cookies and sweets await.*

Above right. *A spray of holly tied with a shimmering bow adds interest to a sconce.*

Osage oranges, variegated English holly, and sprigs of boxwood form a pleasing arrangement on the sideboard at Carter's Grove.

Left. *A rare late eighteenth-century creamware epergne and accessories made at Leeds, England, are displayed on the table in the dining room at the George Wythe House.*

31

Christmas is a time for exchanging special secrets and wishes.

Holly, white pine, and rosemary have been placed in a Worcester porcelain bowl, transfer-printed in cobalt blue, that dates from the third quarter of the eighteenth century.

Dinner guests at a private residence in the Historic Area will be seated at an elegantly arrayed table that features an arrangement of Burfordi holly and statice.

Lemons, limes, lady apples, bayberry, and white pine radiate from a cone of lemons.

33

*Student musicians per-
form in the Music
Teacher's Room. The
mandolin, recorder,
and violin were among
the instruments played
by colonial Virginians.*

34

At Christmas play and make good cheer,
For Christmas comes but once a year.

he annual Christmas exhibit at the Abby Aldrich Rockefeller Folk Art Center is eagerly anticipated. A traditional tree trimmed with unusual handmade ornaments dominates the lobby. Many of these fascinating, one-of-a-kind decorations have been created from natural materials by Williamsburg residents and other friends of the Center.

One gallery features that perennial favorite of holiday visitors, the museum's own dollhouse, which is gaily adorned for the season. Santa and his reindeer-drawn sleigh are perched on the roof. Accompanying the dollhouse is a large selection of antique dolls that includes a remarkable group of English peddler dolls dating from about 1850.

Another gallery is the site of a scaled-up version of a nineteenth-century wooden toy Bavarian village in the museum's collection. Cases concealed in the brightly painted buildings contain hundreds of different German playthings. The village scene is further enlivened by carousel animals, a 290-piece Noah's ark, and other whimsical carvings.

The AARFAC Express, a colorful train built and painted by Colonial Williamsburg artisans, is modeled after a toy in the collection. Young visitors delight in exploring the engine and examining the display of American iron and tin toys in the coach windows. Views of Victorian towns and a facsimile of an 1880 railroad station complete the exhibit.

Elsewhere in the museum, rocking horses, doll carriages, and other antique toys and examples of children's furniture await youngsters and their parents, for whom Christmas wouldn't be Christmas without a visit to the Folk Art Center.

35

The dollhouse is a treasure trove of fascinating miniatures and special holiday touches.

The doll family prepares to celebrate Christmas in the parlor, where garlands of greens, a tiny startopped tree, gaily wrapped packages, and stockings ''hung by the chimney with care'' await.

Antique toys in colorful display cases attract young visitors to the Abby Aldrich Rockefeller Folk Art Center. Hundreds of handmade ornaments decorate the huge spruce, which is festooned with wood shavings chains.

36

The prancing tin pull toy horse was made in New York City during the last quarter of the nineteenth century.

All aboard! Its bell ringing and light flashing, the AARFAC Express is ready to pull away from the station.

A child-sized Bavarian village is the setting for an exhibit of antique toys. These treasured playthings from the past remind today's visitors that Christmas is truly a celebration for the young at heart.

37

The Senior Corps of the Colonial Williamsburg Fifes and Drums steps out proudly.

Left. The siege piece being loaded is an original nine-pounder that dates from the reign of Queen Anne of England.

Below. In the eighteenth century, "firing the Christmas guns" carried holiday greetings across the miles from plantation to plantation. The Charlesville muskets were issued to the Virginia forces after the Franco-American alliance in 1778. Today's young militiamen wear a black and white cockade to commemorate that critical alliance of the American Revolution. In honor of the season, they have added a sprig of mistletoe.

Every child especially enjoys a ride in the oxcart.

Popular among the gentlemen of eighteenth-century Virginia, lawn bowling is enjoyed in Williamsburg again today. The object of the game is to roll the black bowls as close as possible to the small white ball, which is called the jack. After all of the bowls have been rolled, the team whose bowls lie closest to the jack scores points.

40

Snow dusted branches frame the eighteenth-century Powder Magazine.

A snowy day on Duke of Gloucester Street endows the old city with a special kind of quiet charm.

Williamsburg abounds in small details that please the eye. Here snow has frosted the ball and chain that secure an old gate.

43

Snow adorns the stately Coke-Garrett House.

Twiggy branches create pleasing patterns of light and shadow.

The symmetry of eighteenth-century architecture is reflected even in Williamsburg's smaller buildings.

Ice-glazed holly sparkles in the winter sunshine.

45

The table in the Brush-Everard Kitchen holds the best of nature's bounty put by for winter feasting.

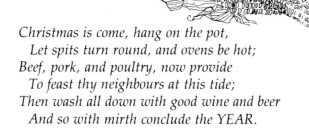

Christmas is come, hang on the pot,
  Let spits turn round, and ovens be hot;
Beef, pork, and poultry, now provide
  To feast thy neighbours at this tide;
Then wash all down with good wine and beer
  And so with mirth conclude the YEAR.

Lavish hospitality is a keynote of the Christmas season in Williamsburg. The eighteenth century was noted for its "groaning boards" laden with the good food and drink that our ancestors so enjoyed. In the Old Dominion, roast beef and venison, Virginia ham, and other local delicacies replaced the traditional boar's head that was the mainstay of the Christmas feast in medieval England. Wild fowl—ducks, geese, turkeys, partridges—abounded in the New World, as did oysters, crabs, clams, mussels, and many kinds of fish, both fresh- and saltwater. Mincemeat pies and plum puddings, fruitcakes and sweetmeats, fruits, nuts, jellies—the hearty appetites of the eighteenth century enjoyed them all, and more. Liquid refreshments were not forgotten either. Virginians' daily beverages included beer, ale, cider, and a variety of wines. Madeira was a favorite fortified wine. The special feasts of Christmas might have called for a toddy or syllabub or for a punch made from rum or brandy. Eggnog, which has become so closely identified with Christmas celebrations, was introduced late in the century.

The hearty good cheer so typical of Christmas in eighteenth-century Virginia is re-created in Williamsburg today. The celebrations combine delicious food with delightful entertainment to provide a treat for all five senses. Enhancing the enjoyment of feasting at the Christmas "groaning boards" are minstrels and madrigal singers, who play and sing the tunes that were popular two hundred years ago. Costumed colonial dancers and the Fifes and Drums perform as well, and all present join in the revelry that marks the holiday season in Williamsburg.

At the Raleigh Tavern Bakery, little fingers pat the dough into the mold just so. The result—spicy gingerbread men!

Inset. The antique walnut cookie mold was made in Europe in the eighteenth century.

*Crowned by a croquembouche de Noël, a lavish display
of desserts to please both eye and palate is arranged in
the Supper Room in the Governor's Palace. Also on the
table are (clockwise): pound cake; fresh fruit of the season;
plum pudding; sweet potato pie; assorted Christmas cookies;
bourbon pecan cake; fresh fruit ambrosia; mocha cake;
marzipan, candied orange peel, and sugar-coated almonds;
sour cherry trifle; and wine jelly mold.*

CHAMPAGNE SHERBET
(1½ quarts)

2 cups sugar
2 cups water
⅔ cup corn syrup
juice of 2 lemons
1 drop yellow food coloring
1 bottle champagne
3 egg whites, unbeaten

Bring the sugar and water to a boil. Add the corn syrup, lemon juice, and food coloring. Cool. Pour the mixture into a large shallow pan, cover, and freeze. When the mixture is frozen, remove it from the refrigerator and let it stand at room temperature for a few minutes. Scrape the mixture into the bowl of a food processor or blender. Mix until smooth. Add the champagne. Return the mixture to the freezer until frozen. Remove and let stand a few minutes. Place ⅓ of the mixture in the bowl of a food processor or blender. Add 1 unbeaten egg white. Mix until smooth. Mix the second ⅓ of the sherbet with 1 unbeaten egg white as above. Repeat with the remaining mixture and egg white. Cover and freeze.

Champagne sherbet would bring any holiday feast to a memorable conclusion.

50

*Eighteenth-century appetites were hearty and dishes were substantial—
roast pork garnished with lady apples, boiled onions, wine jelly mold,
turnips, carrots, and a variety of breads. Soup came steaming hot
from the tureen.*

Tavern fare features fresh sea-food, succulent Virginia ham and roast beef, barbecued ribs, delectable desserts, mugs of foaming ale, and a minstrel's ballads—convivial, sporting, and amorous.

52

A balladeer performs during "gambols" at Chowning's Tavern.

Left. *The table is set for a holiday brunch at a private residence in the Historic Area. The festive centerpiece is a boxwood tree trimmed with hand-decorated Christmas cookies and gay red yarn ribbons. The menu includes shrimp jambalaya, a crisp green salad, and gingerbread men.*

Below. *Pomegranates and boxwood in a basket are a perfect touch for a fireplace.*

54

EGGNOG
(12 cups)

6 eggs, separated
½ cup sugar
2 cups whipping cream
1 cup milk
½ cup bourbon
½ cup brandy
½ cup light rum
nutmeg

Beat the egg yolks with the sugar until thick. Slowly add the cream, milk, and spirits. Chill. Whip the egg whites until soft peaks form and add to the mixture. Chill and let ripen a few hours. Sprinkle with nutmeg before serving.

A nutmeg star tops a bowl of eggnog made the southern way.

Champagne is the libation of choice at a gala New Year's Eve party.
A Stilton cheese and fresh strawberries highlight the lavish collation
that awaits guests at a private residence in the Historic Area.

Cherry, pecan, and mincemeat
tarts are cooling on antique
pewter plates in the pantry at
Carter's Grove plantation.

57

A gigantic Christmas tree graces the entrance hall at Carter's Grove, "the most beautiful house in America."

58

The tree is bedecked with favorite ornaments old and new, popcorn strings, and dozens of tiny white tapers.

The seventeenth-century English artisan Grinling Gibbons was famous for his woodcarvings of plant materials. A modern interpretation above a mantel at Carter's Grove has combined a variety of cones, nuts, and leaves with fresh pomegranates.

A profusion of softly glowing candles creates a festive ambience during a concert in the elegant Governor's Palace ballroom.

60

Music of the season in the parlor of the George Wythe House.

The white pine roping on the mantel is enhanced by holly berries, boxwood, and pine cones. The wreath features the same materials.

61

The Great Hall of the Wren Building at the College of William and Mary is the splendid setting for a recorder trio.

62

At the Grand Illumination of the City, the voices of carolers—soprano and alto, tenor and bass—join in the age-old carols that proclaim the glad holiday tidings.

A holiday concert is in progress at Bruton Parish Church, which is decorated for Christmas with poinsettias, fresh fruit, and greens. The sanctuary looks much as it did when Washington, Jefferson, Randolph, and other notable Virginians worshipped there.

Everyone joins in the revels at the Baron's Feast. Good food and drink and rollicking entertainment highlight a convivial evening.

Garnished with fruits, the boar's head, a traditional Christmas dish in medieval England, is given a modern interpretation.

Madrigal singers perform a variety of eighteenth-century music—catches, carols, and glees.

Now Christmas comes, 'tis fit that we
Should feast and sing, and merry be
Keep open house, let fiddlers play
A fig for cold, sing care away
And may they who thereat repine
On brown Bread and on small beer dine.

The Colonial Games in the gardens of the Governor's Palace are popular with young and old alike . The December air may be nippy, but the participants are so excited that they never feel the slightest chill. Onlookers warm themselves near one of several bonfires whose aromatic wood smoke adds its special fragrance to the convivial gathering.

Activities abound. Children enjoy a cherry pie eating contest and barrel racing. Those who find their way to the center of the Palace maze are rewarded with a cookie. People pitch quoits and pennies, try their hand at lawn bowling and feats of strength, and join the costumed colonial dancers in a reel. Four sturdy young men attempt to climb a greased pole on top of which is a well-filled purse.

When the music of the Fifes and Drums signals the end of the afternoon's events, participants and spectators of all ages feel that they have sampled—if only for a brief time—the simpler pleasures that were such an important part of the lives of Virginians of long ago.

69

A juggler's sleight of hand fascinates his audience.

Pitching pennies into a bucket is more difficult than it appears. Prizes are awarded to those who succeed.

Music was always an important accompaniment to festive occasions in colonial Virginia. Perhaps a piper played in these gardens for the Earl of Dunmore, the Scottish nobleman who was the last royal governor of the colony.

71

Spectators always enjoy the greased pole climb.

72

Climbing the slippery pole is hard work.

The top climber is almost close enough to grasp the purse.

73

Sack racers hop and jump as fast as they can.

74

The cherry pie eating contest is messy but fun.

75

Hoop rolling calls for balance and concentration.

The fiddler's sprightly tunes set toes to tapping, just as they did in colonial Virginia when Colonel William Fitzhugh called in fiddlers who furnished "all the entertainment one could wish for."

In the Palace gardens, ladies and gentlemen in colonial costumes step lightly through the figures of a dance. Soon onlookers will be invited to join in the merriment.

We wish you health, and good fires; victuals, drink, and good stomachs; innocent diversion, and good company; honest trading, and good success; loving courtship, and good wives; and lastly, a merry CHRISTMAS and a happy NEW YEAR.